this too flowed through

a memoir in verse

pat nyman

Legacy Pond Press
939 7th St. W, St Paul, MN 55102
www.beaverspondpress.com

This Too Flowed Through © 2023 by Pat Nyman.
All rights reserved. No part of this book may be reproduced in any form whatsoever, by photography or xerography or by any other means, by broadcast or transmission, by translation into any kind of language, nor by recording electronically or otherwise, without permission in writing from the author, except by a reviewer, who may quote brief passages in critical articles or reviews.

Edited by Alicia Ester
Cover and interior art by Louisa Nyman

ISBN 13: 978-1-64343-654-8
Library of Congress Catalog Number: 2022920276

Printed in the United States of America
First Printing: 2023
27 26 25 24 23   5 4 3 2 1

Book design and typesetting by Tina Brackins

Legacy Pond Press
939 Seventh Street W
St. Paul, MN 55102
www.BeaversPondPress.com

This book is dedicated to
John, Emily, Tan, and Louisa
with my deepest love.

Introduction

I showed up in 1954, spunky, happy, brimming with love.

My sisters and brother were four, six, and eight years older than me; the four of us grew up in a small Midwestern town with my parents. My father was a physician, well liked and respected. He was dedicated to his patients, compassionate, present. A fun-loving guy, he embraced much of life, duck hunting in the early hours of the morning before work, golfing on days off, working on projects in the gardens or around the house, playing poker with the guys and bridge in a couples' group. He warmly loved us kids. We went canoeing, waterskiing, on family trips to the East and the West. He was a responsive father when he was available.

My mother was emotionally and mentally ill, but quite good at disguising it for the outside world. At home, she was exceedingly hard to please, unable to form healthy emotional bonds with us kids, paranoid, and unpredictable, yet powerful. Mom could suck all of the air out of a room. From the earliest years of my life I tried to please her; with my whole little heart, I tried to please her. Never knowing what her responses would be at any given time, I became all too familiar with the feeling of fight, flight, or freeze. Stress hormones coursed through my body daily, and I learned to be hypervigilant. It wasn't until my twenties that I began to understand our mother was ill. Until then, she was just our mother, that's how she was, and as children do, I assumed all of it was my fault.

From my earliest moments, I learned that who we are is not always embraced, that innocence is not protection, that love is not always met with love.

Over the years I have written a number of poems about this situation and my relationship with my mother. They address my anger, my sadness, and the loneliness of growing up unseen.

A diagnosis of breast cancer in 2000, and the surgeries that followed, were tectonic shifts for me. My body was no longer familiar and comfortable. My psyche and emotions shifted from hour to hour. Not to be left behind, my heart and soul jumped into the fray compelling me to take a deep look at what I had believed up to that point about myself, my spiritual values, my life.

Overwhelmed by the amount of healing that needed to occur, within six months I became highly anxious and depressed. It was a dark time for me. Someone else might have made changes in baby steps and perhaps had a smoother path. That is not how I was made. If there is something to be dealt with, I plunge in. This is part me, part what I absorbed from my environment growing up. I learned early to be watchful and fix what could be fixed; there was likely something else coming. I became used to working on myself, tirelessly searching for the elusive formula that might win my mother's acceptance and love.

Life has its dark places and unwanted surprises. Most of us push hard against news we don't want, reacting strongly when we are buffeted around by things we can't control. Yet I have also known countless moments of exquisite joy and richness.

Much of this book is about the challenges I have moved through, as writing has been a means for me to process what life has offered up, a way to come to terms with its pain and its blessings. Both have been richly woven into my life; I consider myself abundantly fortunate.

Compiling these poems is meant to be helpful in some way, perhaps to allow you to feel hope as you experience another's budding awareness and evolution, or to find kinship in a similar challenge you have faced.

In gratitude and love,

Pat Nyman
December 2022

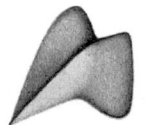

Table of Contents

I Can't Remember 1
Kindergarten Phobia, 1959 3
Fourth-Grade Sick Day 5
If I Were to Allow Myself to Be Very Angry,
　　What Would Make the List? 7
Coloring Inside the Lines 9
Train Whistle, Red Lights 12

What We Missed 13
Decided to Stop 15
RAGE 17
RAGE 2 18
What If You Didn't Want to Be a Mother? . . . 20
I Wonder 22
I'm Grateful, Mom 24
Mother's Day, 2018 26
This Earth's Mothers 28

Elegy (2000) 31
Breast Cancer 33
High Anxiety 35
Loss 37
Dark Lover 38
Storm on the Lake 39
Elegy to My Breasts 41
Travelogue 43

Why Did You Leave? (2002) 45
December 10, 2002 47
Aunt's Lament 49
In Memoriam 50
Dear Liz 52

One Cell's Mutation (2019) 53
Mean Survival Ten to Twelve Years 55
I'm Not Afraid to Die 56
Breakfast at the Log House Lodge 57
Why Now? 58
Unmutated IGHV 60

Learning 63
The Beach 65
Becoming. 67
Time. 69
The Circle 70
In Between 72
What the Trees Know 73
Orion's Lesson. 75
A Recipe for Finding Oneself 76
No Small Thing 78
Most in Need of Forgiveness 80
Retraining My Brain. 82
A Blank Page. 84
Free Stuff. 86
Blue Sky. 87
Landing Here 88
Indigenous People's Day. 90
Breathe In 92
My Sister's Meditation 94
What I Do Know 96

Much to Celebrate 99
Twentieth Anniversary. 101
Fiftieth Birthday 103
A Toast to Dorothea 105
The Gift of Ginny 108
Threshold/Thirtieth Birthday 110

Unsuspecting, Unprepared 111
Gotta Get This Down. 113
What Will Come of This Pandemic?. 117
The Beforetime .119

Lost and Found 123
Child's Face. 125
Butterfly in Chains 126

Mindful or Mindless	128
Reach Out	130
If I Should Die	131
The Grace in Writing, a Sestina Practice	132
Dad and Uncle Bill	134
This Sadness	136
Graceport Walk	138
Little Oak	139
The Venus of Willendorf	140
Snowfall	141
Brain's First Minute	142
Morning Walk	143
Meditation	145
Mid-October Day	146
Beauty	147
Saturday	148
Home	149
Black Cotton Dress	150

I Can't Remember

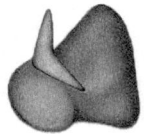

Kindergarten Phobia, 1959

She knows sweaty little boys chased
grade school girls whose panties showed
from atop the monkey bars.
But she can't remember
any gestures or words
that made their way to her
as she leaned into the playground fence
and called to her mother
mailing letters
at the post office just across the street.

She can't remember how many times
her older sister was summoned
from her fourth-grade class
where Miss Smith wrote on the blackboard
with part of her third finger missing
to meet her outside her kindergarten door
and talk to her in urgent tones
to convince her to stay.

When did her mother come
and park the gray Buick station wagon
    with the white top
up against the curb?
How many times did she sit in that car
and dread going back
where classmates squirmed on rest mats
and tried to look up Mrs. Heller's dress as she passed,
and after a while took their chocolate goiter pills
with half-pint cartons of milk?

She doesn't remember the feeling in her stomach
as she walked back across the concrete
with its chalked-in foursquare plots,
or the shaking in her legs
as she climbed down the speckled terrazzo steps
to her kindergarten classroom on the right.

She doesn't remember struggling to ignore
all of the heads turning
to look
and the noisy chatter
that stopped
as she opened the door
to try again.

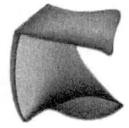

Fourth-Grade Sick Day

Naked trees framed the world outside,
dark vees of geese across the bleak, gray sky.
Pajamas soft against my skin,
I smelled of Tide and the sourness of fever,
nestled into my pillow on the couch in the den
as my classmates propped open their desks
to look for red-orange, burnt sienna, or cerulean.

Bob Barker's "Come on down!"
to a portly woman in aqua
was interrupted by the serious voices of
men in dark suits,
their eyes fixed on me
as they delivered their confusing news.
Then a pot-bellied man in a maroon leisure suit
and two giddy women in bright polyester blouses
guessed the price of a new RCA color TV.
The dark suits came back
with images of a couple in a convertible
waving back and forth in the morning sun,
until they weren't.

The lady in aqua had come closest
to the price of the TV,
and moved on to a spinning game
to win the green Naugahyde chair and ottoman,
dreams of her living room transformed.
Again, the men returned.

I could hear my parents' quiet tones
as they ate lunch in the kitchen.
They didn't know,
had no idea.
I ran to them announcing
"The president has been shot!"
"You heard what?!"
"Oh, I don't think so, Patti."

I led them back to the den
where the talking, talking men
had now taken over
all of the TV channels,
repeating the news over and over and over.
I thought of my friends, my teacher,
my sisters and brother
all at school,
and I felt grown up and important.

If I Were to Allow Myself to Be Very Angry, What Would Make the List?

My six-year-old sister's
sweet care
during my infancy,
ten-pound body hefted down the stairs,
bottles warmed on the stove,
diapers changed.
Where was my mother?

Kindergarten phobia that I can't recall,
insistence that I go back in.
No warm and loving arms of comfort,
no professional help.
How did I do this day after day?

Calling out to say hello,
watching her ignore me.
She paused for a moment,
I knew she heard.
Didn't I exist?

Sleepless in grade school,
facing the nights alone,
no one to soften the anxiety,
to hold me close.
Who would walk through this with me?

Home from school, I'd ask
"Can I tell you something?"
Seeker of absolution for
tiny childhood transgressions,
hoping for release and
the feeling of being OK.
So young, so troubled,
so alone.
Was there something wrong with me?

After a date, tiptoeing up the stairs
so she couldn't hear my return,
subject me to questions
that shouldn't be asked.
Wasn't I entitled to privacy?

Being made to apologize
when nothing was my fault
in order to keep the peace,
to keep us all moving forward.
Where was taking responsibility?
Where was truth?

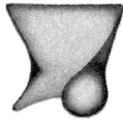

Coloring Inside the Lines

Perfect pages
in my coloring book,
nothing outside the lines.
Upper and lowercase letters
rounded and smooth,
loops and curves precise.
My dresser top a regiment,
crayons standing
straight on end,
blues and purples for eyeshadow,
reds and pinks for lipstick or rouge.
Don't touch.
Don't topple.
Realign.
Breathe out.

Daily I recited my list
of things done wrong,
might possibly have done wrong,
fleetingly thought about doing wrong.
Her response
was impatience.
And when I couldn't sleep,
little mind haunted
by imagined transgressions,
and outsized fears,
she was annoyed.

I can't remember
her arms around me,
pulling me
into the warmth
of her body,
or an unhurried back rub
by gentle hands
making things right,
easing the transition to sleep.

My high school sisters
consistently had plans,
all of them important
it seemed.
This time I ran
up the stairs
and slammed my door,
left out again,
too young
to be included,
old enough
to feel excluded.
It felt good
to watch my mother
try to comfort me,
good to express my hurt,
good to shut her out.

I ironed
my dad's T-shirts,
smoothed out
his underwear,
the soft cotton warm
under my hands.
I breathed in
the fresh hot smell
as the iron
pushed out all the wrinkles.
I knew the flat folds
would never be quite right,
never good enough
for her.

If only I could say
the right things,
get straight A's,
fourth child
coming through
trying to fit
the mold.
I meant to stand tall,
I meant to be thin,
power through ten-mile bike rides,
swim to the bridge,
execute two hundred sit-ups.
I meant to be attractive,
wear blouses
with Peter Pan collars,
Villager skirts and sweaters.

It never worked.

Train Whistle, Red Lights

I lay in bed
not moving.
I had checked for wolves under the bed
and slippery monsters in the closet
leaped to the mattress
from halfway across the room.
One never knows.
One just never knows.

I heard the train whistle
far off in the distance,
so mournful
I could barely breathe.
As it sounded its low, sad notes
it seemed like a song
I had long known by heart.

The window across from the foot of my bed
framed the darkening sky
as I lay in my bed waiting for sleep.
I could see the blinking red lights
on the radio tower across the river.
Over and over they repeated
    I see you.
        I am here.
            I see you.

What We Missed

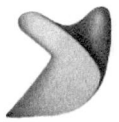

Decided to Stop

I've decided to stop trying
whether it's a matter of survival
or a steep learning curve,
it's time.

Time to know that
a lifetime of trying is enough.
Trying to be seen.
Trying to be heard.
Trying to be enough.
Trying to be who you wanted me to be.

I'm no longer angry
that in all my offerings
nothing was good enough,
that your eyes often held a look of disgust
now imprinted on my soul,
that you were busy
making sure who I should not become,
that I can't remember one time
when you held me
just to feel my body close to yours,
to feel the wonder of your child.

I'm no longer angry,
but sadness lives in every cell in my body.
Sadness that I never had a mother
who delighted in watching me grow,
sadness that I've walked through my life
looking for love,
unable to trust when it is there,
sadness that I've been afraid,
seeking a solid place,
a way to be in the world that might work.

I will still love you,
for you are my mother.
I will forgive the things
that can't be changed.
I will be gentle and honest
for that is who I am,
and I will share moments with you.
But I will no longer hope.
I've decided to stop trying.

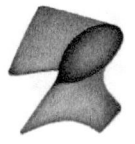

RAGE

Consumed by staggering
harsh
steely-eyed
desire-to-destroy
screaming
resentful
storms of hate
ranting questions
no answers
rage.

Can I hate for just a while,
let it crackle in my bones
and rankle my heart,
this outrage,
this thing I didn't seek,
this violation of my soul?

Or will I accept
what has happened
with love?
See with the eyes
of compassion?

Can I hold both,
this rage at injustice
and love's understanding?

There might be an explosion
building in my head.

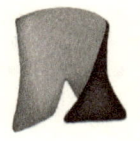

RAGE 2

Perhaps I want to
rend the world apart
clawing it open
to a dark endless pit
like the bottomless hole
in my heart.

Or smash something's head
into a thousand bony shards
like the edgy spaces
in my brain,
endlessly searching for answers,
watchful,
restless,
anxious.

Or cause blindness in a most horrific way,
perhaps acid would work.
Because I could never see,
was always kept from seeing,
groping
to find solid ground and
a self I could recognize.

And what about evisceration?
Most despicable of all thoughts
this tearing out of one's innards,
one's most hidden, private functions.
But, yes,
I have been eviscerated,
my soul slashed
stomped on and
laughed at,
met with disgust.

Fire might be good,
intense and hot, very hot.
I was consumed by flames,
by a blaze so white
it left only ashes
in its path,
a few embers
that glowed small
but bright,
off to the side
until they could be stirred up,
coaxed and
breathed back to life.

Something needs to be taught a lesson.

What If You Didn't Want to Be a Mother?

What if you didn't want to surrender your body,
share it completely with this other
that depended on you
for its growth, its safety, its life?

What if you loved your body as it was,
your beauty an interface with the world,
familiar and dependable,
predictable,
yours?

What if you were pregnant
with no choice about giving birth?
What if you were frightened
of what you would have to endure,
this birth and beyond?

What if you were not drawn to babies?
What if it was hard to connect
with this fragile being,
hard to meet the endless demands,
hard to form a bond?

What if you couldn't hang onto yourself
and give your children what they needed?
What if it was a struggle for you
to get through each day?

What if you cared
but had a hard time showing it?
What if you felt more
than it seemed?
What if you wished
you could look in my eyes
and give me a long, tight hug,
saving some of that love
for yourself?
What if you took the leap
and told me you loved me?

I Wonder

I wonder why
you decided to have children.
Was it a product of the times,
that expectation of
a lovely home,
a successful husband,
a suitable number of children?

I wonder if
when you gazed
into your eyes
at the mirror,
you knew
that this was over your head,
overwhelming,
not what you could do?

Did you know
it would be hard to connect,
that you would be incapable
of forming the bond
that an infant,
a small child,
a person needs
to grow and thrive?

I wonder if
each successive child
brought on more panic,
pushed you further
into yourself,
created resentment
that your life
felt no longer yours.

I wonder when
you knew
you didn't feel whole,
and maybe worried
that you shouldn't proceed,
but did anyway.
I wonder if
you were intensely lonely,
unable to let anyone in
or allow yourself
to connect.
I wonder if you knew
that for decades
connections were difficult for me,
and that loneliness
was the cloak I wore daily?

I wonder if you knew
your power was not in
what you thought
you controlled,
but in what you were unable to give.

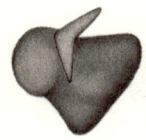

I'm Grateful, Mom

There were so many years
    when I didn't understand,
    let myself believe your mothering
    was the only kind,
    that because you didn't know
    how to love,
    I was unlovable.

There were many, many years
    when I reacted,
    thought my story
    was about you,
    when my emotions
    raged and ruled.

Then there were years,
    many years
    after I awoke,
    and realized
    I was in charge,
    and could create
    my own story.

More lately there have been years
    of looking at you
    and seeing you
    less as a mother,
    more as a deeply
    troubled person,
    a tortured soul.

You moved on September twenty-ninth,
    rest your weary soul.
    Now the years
    will be steeped
    in the knowledge that
    I was a good student, that
    you taught me a lot
    about mothering.
    I am so grateful
    you taught me how to love.

Mother's Day, 2018

Thank you
for carrying my tiny body
in yours
developing minute by minute, hour by hour
for nine long months.
Thank you for helping me enter this world
red and crying, longing
for that safe darkness
from which I had come.

Thank you for keeping me fed,
keeping me clothed,
keeping me safe.

Thank you for all I learned because of
what you were unable to teach:
that babies need to be seen,
that connection establishes trust,
that each one of us is unique,
that our ability to love comes from being loved.

There have been other teachers—
a loving husband,
three cherished children,
siblings and friends,
counselors, books, spiritual guides.
The work has taken me to the edge,
allowed no free passes,
yet always provided
who and what I needed.

In the end,
there is love
in the lilies-of-the-valley
with their delicate fragrance,
the cardinal's brilliant song,
the trickle of a nearby brook.
There is the opening of a heart
long closed in fear,
the ability to look in the mirror
and see goodness,
the willingness to be curious.

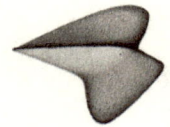

This Earth's Mothers

Say you realized you weren't really wanted,
this fresh, sweet, frisky newborn.
It was just too much for your mother
while she was pregnant,
and after you arrived.
What then?

You'd turn to the ocean
to show you the rhythm of breathing,
a moving in and moving out
that connects you
to the earth, the moon, the stars.

You'd look to the trees
to teach you rootedness,
and strength,
patience,
how to stand tall
and weather a storm.

The stars would guide you
to shine brightly,
rest in stillness and
wait until things become clear,
to be at peace.

The passionflower would instruct you
on beauty and attention to detail,
trusting the wisdom
in the passing of the seasons,
and allowing the universe to
hold you up.

You'd look to the sky
and understand openness
and generosity,
that the clouds always move on,
yet the sky remains.

And then you'd discover the light
in your own heart,
that you were created
to be just as you are,
that you have all that you need.

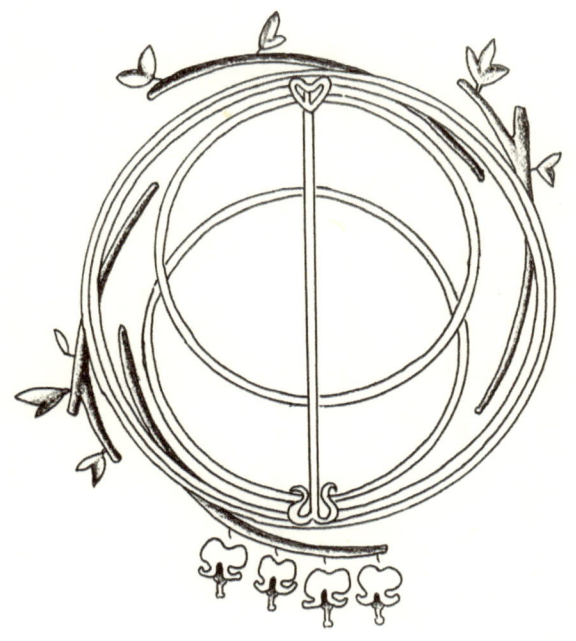

Elegy
2000

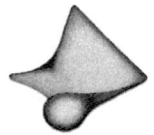

Breast Cancer

The gift was delivered on a usual day,
a dark surprise
left on the doorstep.
I longed to return it,
tell someone it couldn't be accepted.
But it was too late.

The gift possessed me,
overwhelmed my thoughts
and controlled my actions,
led me down one path,
then another,
desperate to weave
it into the fabric
of the comfortable life
I had been living.

Voices declared their advice
in the names of affection and love,
they swirled through my mind,
tangling my own answers
in a web of well-meant concern,
perspectives tried on
against the backdrop of the future.

A tiny light illuminated my path
clear and brilliant in its knowing.
It took me into the pain
to meet the unknown.

I now know why the gift was sent,
to look inside
and stand in awe of all I find,
to accept this gift just as it was given,
to feel gratitude.

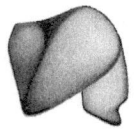

High Anxiety

Air fills only the largest
parts of my lungs
and I gasp again,
straining to breathe.

I cannot trust
my next step,
interaction,
the next breath.
Living has become charged as
adrenaline courses through my body
and convinces me to be afraid.

Thoughts flit by,
fears to assess,
dark possibilities,
circling back to the start,
accelerating with each new attempt
to reign them in.

My body quivers
on high alert,
sleep an unattainable goal,
this wakefulness a nightmare
that can't be turned off.

My body has betrayed me,
my stomach won't settle
heart throbs out of control
hands damp with fight-or-flight
breathing so shallow
I strain to go deeper.

Perhaps it's not there now,
I'll just check.
And for the millionth time today
I gasp for air,
feel the pervasive buzzing,
and try to attempt
a semblance of control.

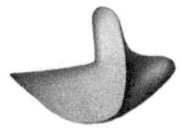

Loss

Tears erupt and spill over
undesired, unplanned.
Overwhelmed again
by an exquisite sadness
I cannot control.

My body is mine, yet not.
I long for the comfort of
knowing it well again,
to sink into the predictability
of its responses
and the safety of its form.

Breast cancer
rearranged the entire landscape,
womb removed within months.
No chance of creating a new life.
No room to protect a growing form.
No breasts to nourish a new babe.

My tears are salty,
my cheeks wet,
this emptiness continues
to fill me
and pull me down.

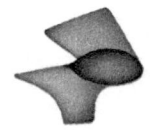

Dark Lover

He chants
    lost hope, nothing to lose,
        gray notes
            seductive,
                pulsating.

Darkness descends
        shrouding every cell,
            pulling me under
                the covers where
    I
    can't
    breathe.

As the darkness
    swirls and multiplies
I surrender
    to his sinister
            embrace.

Our bed has become
    my grave
        I sink in deeper
    pleading
        to be taken,
            no longer having to wait.

Storm on the Lake

A storm has blown up on the lake overnight.
Minutes ago
its surface
all stillness and calm,
reflection of expansive sky,
soaring birds, rooted trees.
Now it acts agitated,
difficult to manage.
Where things were clear,
they are now muddy.
Where sunlight danced,
darkness looms,
and where soft breezes caressed the water,
rough winds now pull and tear.

Lightning flashes anxiously
competing energies pulling this way and that.
Confusion reigns.

But then I remember
that place of calm
deep below the surface
where the turbulence of emotion
and the undulations of thought
cannot reach.
There is a total clarity
that can only be felt instead of seen,
and a complete stillness
that brings peace.

Storms cannot be controlled, I know,
nor the seasons of a life.
But one can try to remember
that place of calm within.
It is a gift connecting us
to every other soul
who is trying to remember.

Elegy to My Breasts

The milk stain spreads
across my dark blouse,
a prickling sensation
then a warm fullness
and release.
This nectar
a private sacrament in
our self-sufficient world.
As you suckle, my little one,
our eyes meet and lock.

But no longer.

The soft fullness of
these curves await
the touch of your
strong hands, and
my back arches as
you pull on puckered skin,
your mouth opening
places I want
filled.

But no longer.

Under steaming water
I lather my hands with
lavender soap,
they slide across my body,
this body that
gives shape
to my image.

But no longer.

I wake
on a surgical bed,
both breasts
removed
by cold steel instruments
to be dissected
in a pathology lab.

Caress these new forms.
    They are trying
    their hardest
    to become something
    they are not.

Travelogue

I was gone for months
living out of a suitcase of
borrowed metaphors.

I dulled my pain with prescriptions,
and took in the food brought by concerned friends.
I read the stories of other travelers,
and welcomed the deep unconsciousness of sleep.
I listened to wise advice
and heard about my good luck,
that things could have been much worse.

I grew weary of my travels
and trying to find the meaning in
following someone else's itinerary.
My old maps were obsolete and useless.

I found my compass in a
secret place in the suitcase
and began to divine my own way.
A stream nearby flowed gently along its course,
and the sunset held quiet peace.
The stars came out that night,
bright pinpoints of eternity.

I emptied my suitcase
tucking each item where it can be found
should I need it again.
Then I turned to watch the dusk
transform each branch
on the tree outside my window
into an exquisite masterpiece.

Why Did You Leave?
2002

December 10, 2002

An explosive crack.
Another.
Time stops.
Sits massive
    on our chests.
Air inhaled
    only as gasps.

Time ties itself in knots
    curling around
    pudgy hands
    gripping a new pencil,
    or proudly holding a basketball
    just before a shot,
now pulling us
    forward to a
bed that won't be slept in,
hills she won't climb,
eyes she won't meet.

We are holding tightly
    to times
when we could see
your bright light,
Liz.

In the echo of
    that loud crack
there is a place
where questions hang
in the air,
elusive shapes
    and colors
flitting back and forth
    with no place
    to settle.

The knot grows tighter,
    larger.
Strands tangle
as they try to weave
    some familiar pattern.

So we must breathe . . .
    breathe again,
    breathe yet again.
Feel our hearts
    straining
    toward yours.

Aunt's Lament

Your mother's primeval moan
arises from the depth
of her aching womb,
starts low and crescendos
filling all space everywhere.

Your father's strong arms
hang limp at his sides
stripped of dreams and plans.

> Liz, why did you leave
> so early, so young
> to make your December grave
> up the trail
> through the woods
> past your favorite old tree?
>
> Why did you leave
> just when the snow
> was sparkling in the sun,
> and I could've made us
> mugs of hot coffee
> and crisp toast with tart cherry jam
> while we talked
> of nothing
>   and everything that matters?
>
> How did you know it was time?
>   The edge of the air?
>   The angle of the sun?
>   The weight of the gun in your hand?

In Memoriam

I can't remember seeing you stand at the free throw line with your knees slightly bent, or the expression on your face when you missed the shot . . . or when you didn't.

I can't remember your hands fingering nuggets of topaz or sparkling facets of amethyst as you gave another necklace your creative flourish.

Did you pull on your stained jeans and slide into your tennis shoes without laces to change the oil in that old car you bought to teach yourself auto mechanics? Were the creases in your hands defined by the black of oil and grease when you finished?

I can't hear the sound of your voice when you were six or seven and how it demanded respect from every one of us aunts and uncles at the cabin. Or how we stepped out of your way because you knew what game we should play next, or where we should take our walk, or when we should have dinner.

Why can't I remember what I had for lunch the day we tiptoed around topics of God and the universe and how we might determine some of our own reality? What shirt were you wearing? What earrings danced on your ears as you took a bite of your bagel or swallowed some of your fruit juice? And was your hair pulled back in a ponytail or gently drifting back and forth as you listened to me and then spoke your eighteen-going-on-forty-year-old mind?

I can't remember the day or the hour I realized we had a special bond as aunt and niece, or the tiniest quickening I would feel in my stomach when my email originated from liz@hotmail.com.

Was it cloudy that day we went shopping to buy you something fun, my small gesture of gratitude for the time you spent caring for me after my surgeries for breast cancer? Did we stop and browse at American Eagle and Express and The Limited, or was the orange and hot pink skirt clearly the one from the start?

I can't see your face when you weren't smiling, or the curve of your jaw as it met your neck. And I can't remember a time when you didn't jump into each day, galloping through the house to wake your cousin for a surprise breakfast at Perkins, or looking straight into my eyes as we savored steaming lattes.

Panic inches up my chest and into my throat because I know that someday I will have trouble seeing you. How will I picture the shape of your fingernails or the edges of the muscles in your arms? I won't be able to feel your body against mine in a loving hug. The bed you slept in at our house won't be warm in the morning, and the sheets will never smell like you again. I won't hear the exuberance of your laugh, and it may take a split second longer for your face to become clear.

What then?

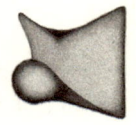

Dear Liz

Dear Liz,
how was it for you?
What took you away so soon,
so young?
What despair overwhelmed you,
and sucked all your hope away?

When did you know
you couldn't go on,
and switch from trying to stay
to making plans to leave?
Were you unsure as you got ready, or
was it easy in the end?

Was your brain muddled
and your heart broken?
Were you confused and agitated,
or did you feel clarity and purpose?
Do you wish you could do it over,
stay awhile,
see what might've happened?

For us it is still hard to accept
that cold December day.
We feel only what-ifs
and if-onlys
and deep, deep loss.

What is it like for you?

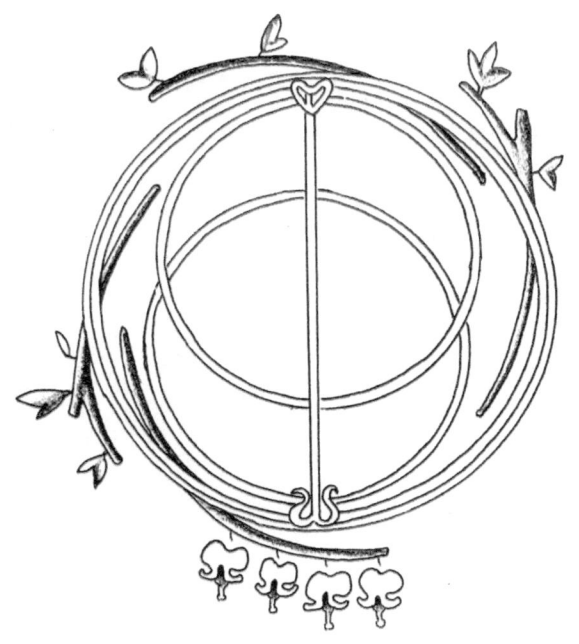

One Cell's Mutation
2019

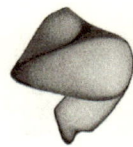

Mean Survival Ten to Twelve Years

Statistics are statistics.
But they are statistics.
They are informative
straightforward
useful,
until it is you.

Monoclonal B-cell
Chronic lymphocytic leukemia
Unmutated IGHV
Trisomy 12

Median survival ten to twelve years.

Reduced to numbers.

Hit by a truck.

Worldview and world shifts
to something less certain
something more focused
something more beautiful.

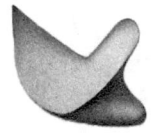

I'm Not Afraid to Die

I'm not afraid to die.
I know I will be embraced
by a love so large
that I will know
it would've been better
to have hurt less,
loved more,
to have spent this life
pursuing beauty.

But what if there isn't enough time
to feel my breasts and belly
against the curve
of your strong warm back,
to know the sweet longing
of my body responding
to your familiar, sensuous hands,
to look into your bluest
of blue eyes
and see that soul that I love,
to dance in your arms
with our bodies so close
that there is no space
between us?

Heart races,
breath shallow.

What if there's not enough time?

Breathe in, four counts.
Breathe out, to the count of eight.

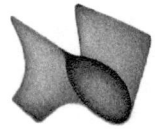

Breakfast at the Log House Lodge

It's September 27
and we are having a lovely breakfast
at our lodge in Three Rivers, California.
Our host happens to mention that
her husband has CLL,
diagnosed eight years ago,
and with the exception of the first,
none of the medications has worked.

We held this information
in our bellies
and tight in our lungs
as we walked through
the sequoia forests.

The trees, standing tall,
trunks mammoth,
created a sacred space
where things can live
for 3,000 years
thriving
despite fire
despite wind and storms
despite drought
despite everything.

I walked
among the trees
feeling their strength
and their timelessness
and decided
things flourish
in their own time.

Why Now?

Why now?

I have just settled in
with this more whole self,
a bit lighter and more aware,
less encumbered,
less hooked and
driven by anxiety.

Why the fuck now?

This emotional and spiritual
healing
took a long time,
a very long time
to see and understand,
stop grasping,
wanting it all to be another way,
needing to control
and be right,
desperate grabs at peace.

Why now?

This coming together,
pieces fitting snugly into their places,
is nothing short of victory,
chains broken and
things allowed to breathe,
connections deep instead of fraught,
ease and
joy,
and understanding.

Why now?

Just when I have done
so much work,
decades of work,
becoming this person
instead of that,
this one
who is free
and open
and grateful
and present.

The timing is perfect.

Unmutated IGHV

Having CLL
was supposed to be
easy,
way off in the distance
and not so hard, even then.

Loved ones remark:
"Oh, I know someone
who has that,
they've had it
for a very long time,
decades in fact,"
implying that my experience
will be the same,
hoping that my experience
will be the same,
understandably glad it's not them.

The initial blood work
that told my CLL story
included some scary characters:
the three-headed monster, Trisomy 12,
and the dreaded, devouring
unmutated IGHV.

Why me?
But life responds,
as do my soul and heart and mind,
Why not me?

Unmutated sounds like a good thing,
right?
Mutations get us into trouble.
But unmutated refers to
an inability to shift and
meet challenges.
Really?
I feel so very much more flexible
and healthy
these last years.

Scientists tell us that
the environment in our bodies
that existed in the past
has a large impact
on what happens in the present.

There were large amounts of cortisol
and adrenaline
coursing through my blood
for so many years
they're hard to count,
protecting my body
from existing or potential threats,
until the protection became the threat.

Learning

The Beach

I am on the beach.

Waves roll in and wash out,
reminding me of my past and
cleansing me of its limiting powers,
treasures left behind to be sifted,
delicate fragments and thick shells,
walls guarding inner vulnerabilities.
Iridescent, shining shapes beckon,
each a creation to celebrate,
as I am beginning to know I am.

Smooth, weathered shells
rubbed clean by the hands of time,
spiny dramatic shapes fascinate,
unique and colorful,
delicate, translucent forms.
I see myself in them all,
each one calls
        "Treasure me,
        find that part of you where
        we are one."

Birds soar and dip, scurry and cry
flying with the triumph of movement
and their fortune at being fed by the sea.
I soar with them,
notice every movement's impact
on what happens next.

I look to the sea.
Its motion calms me.
I answer with the rhythm of my breathing.
There are dark depths
and hidden terrors in the sea
but I sense if I can flow in and out,
I will be brought to shore.

I am on the beach.
I am the beach.

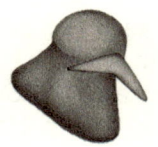

Becoming

Please don't say "You should try this."
It only gets added to the debate in my head
and I might listen more because it is you.

Please don't say "Have you ever thought of being that?"
I've never felt free to think of being anything
pulled this way and that by messages
whispering from another place and time.

Please don't make my choices for me
what music to dance to,
what food to taste,
what color to wear,
the fragrance for my bath.
Each one becomes, for me,
a beginning sketch
of who I am.

This fragile seed
is just beginning to grow.
It needs space and light and time.
It's taken this long
to break through the outer shell,
this long to feel the possibility of growth.

As the days unfold,
I am nourished by everything,
holding out their offerings in turn
flowing in and out of awareness
until we merge or not.

And then, as with a flower, I realize
everything I need is right here
waiting to be discovered and honored,
emerging bit by bit when I am calm
gently, yet persistently,
pushing to the surface and light.

Time

We seem to measure time
by whether we have spent
our past
the way we would've hoped
or whether we will have enough time
in the future
to do everything we want.

We are focused
on time's passing,
the fear that
whatever time we have
could never be enough.

Measure time instead by
sunlight streaming in the window, coaxing you awake
the snowflake that settles gently on your sleeve
the softness of a lover's conscious kiss
the wind in your hair on a clear, spring day.

Measure your time by
the touch of your cheek against that of your child
the sound of laughter shared with friends
a well-prepared meal eaten slowly by candlelight
the music of a master that speaks to your heart.

The Circle

Didn't you know
that you arrived
just the way you were
as a gift to the universe,
your untouched soul
a blessing
to this waiting earth?

Didn't you know
that the first time you opened your eyes,
reached out with a tiny hand,
or cried out to be heard,
you were still pure and unspoiled?

Then the march of time began.
Seeds of doubt crept in
and questions arose.
Your choices were often made for you
in a world made by those
whose choices were often made for them.
Your light still burned bright,
now haunted by a growing shadow.

A thousand voices shouted their shoulds
and convictions, claiming
they knew exactly what would be right
for you in this life.
Didn't they know you already possessed
a delicate kernel of knowing
from the very beginning?

Then you joined the parade,
marching this way and that
following orders, standing straight,
making sure to keep yourself in line,
all the while the glow within
getting dimmer,
waiting out the storm
behind ever stronger walls and barricades.
Didn't you know?

At the point furthest from home
you turned a corner
and began to feel a longing,
yearning for something beyond
the rank and file and order
that had kept your life on course thus far.
Didn't you know that your journey
would bring you back home?

Inside, a voice whispered softly,
you are the gift,
without appearances, explanations, or excuses.
As you shed the structures that
took you far from home,
you were guided to the present
and coaxed to your next awareness.

Gentle hands reach out
enfolding you in love,
teaching you to trust your light.
Don't you know you are here
exactly the way you are
as your perfect offering to the dance?

In Between

birth and death

light and darkness

responsibility and freedom

forty-eight and forty-nine

energy and exhaustion

security and fear

connection and distance

yesterday and today

confusion and understanding

today and tomorrow

joy and pain

winter and spring

impatience and compassion

I want to live the ands,
not reaching for what lies on either side,
not defining life by boundaries.

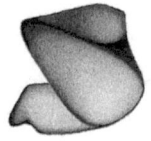

What the Trees Know

Stand tall, and let your roots run deep.
Reach out and up, ever growing and opening
but stay firmly rooted to your place.

Be strong, with the strength to withstand all the storms
that will come your way,
yet be flexible and bend as needed.

Take only what you truly need.
Provide what you are able to provide.
Don't be afraid to let parts of yourself die
as you make way for the new and unknown.

Embrace periods of rest and savor stillness,
stretching always toward the light,
and the wide open sky.

Communicate with others freely
as you create an interconnected web
that extends far and wide.
Be completely yourself,
knowing that you never could
be anything else.

Be a safe haven to others
holding space as they find their way,
a shelter in their woundedness,
or a place to sing with exquisite joy.

Drink in the gifts of each new day
the warmth of the sun, a fresh splash of rain,
the soft touch of another's skin,
the wild abandon of dancing in the wind.

And, as you age, and return to the earth's
    welcoming embrace
hold close all that has gone before,
and know the rich offering of your place in time.

Orion's Lesson

It happened a number of years ago
on a crystal clear, bracing winter's night.
Looking up, I saw Orion
almost close enough to touch,
and oh, so bright.

The stars in his belt drew me,
one in particular
whose light shone radiant and true.
It was hard to leave,
to move on from that moment
of connection.

As I stood in the quiet,
drawn to the star's beauty,
it began to quietly teach me
to let my light shine
as if I had no other choice,
to practice silence
and reverence,
to be steady,
promote peace and stillness,
and know that I am part of something timeless,
reaching into the distant past and
the unknown future.

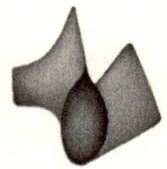

A Recipe for Finding Oneself

Care about yourself, really care.
Do the things you love
sleeping late deep under soft covers
inhaling the aroma of coffee
soaking in a bath with candlelight's glow
feeling your feet on a pine forest's path.

Listen to your body.
It wants to tell you what it needs.
Eat good things when you are hungry.
Quench your thirst.
Create movement often.
Rest when you are weary, or sooner.
Value this body, your lifelong companion,
caress it softly,
whisper your gratitude.

Honor silence
practice listening,
open and receptive.
Look into your own eyes,
and see who is really there
beyond the agendas, emotions, and chatter.
Meet your eyes again.

Be open to awe.
A dark night sky filled with bright stars
whose light and quiet presence
teach of timelessness and holding one's place,
the exquisite beauty of an unfolding flower,
petals at once delicate and powerful,
the majesty of trees
who've stood their ground for millennia,
made from the stories of man, animal, climate.

Touch joy
in laughter's easy release,
the playfulness of a dog,
dancing with wild abandon,
being held in your family's embrace.

Understand that you are here
to be yourself,
to experience
through your unique lens,
to honor
what you have been given.

No Small Thing

In these days
when truth is a mirage,
and we live our lives
certain that we know
what is right,
there is a danger
of seeing each other
as the other,
of citing reasons
to rally behind our tribe,
safe behind its beliefs,
searching for those exchanges
that keep us in our places.

Watch out
lest we become hardened,
unable to see
the pain of the other's loss,
the lightness in their joy,
the striving to find meaning
that is also their struggle.
Watch out
lest we define the world
by our narrow perspectives
and limited experience,
proclaiming that we care deeply.

And how to help the world
in our small way,
when our hearts
crave justice and truth?
A teacher explained:
Give to the world
what you think you most need.

As you approach another
in a shop or on the street,
lift your chin and
look into their eyes
with gentleness, with curiosity.
This is no small thing.

Most in Need of Forgiveness

For the abandonment
beginning in your womb,
mother,
little ability
to bond or
respond
to your innocent babe.

For the little slights
on the playground
as I jostled
for attention
and thought it important
to aim for the top.

For the calculated cruelties
of girlhood adolescence
most often uttered
behind the other's back.

For kindnesses
I could have spoken
but didn't.

For our twenty-something divorce,
the unintended hurt
of wanting
to be free,
wanting someone else.
For my determination
that must have cut deep.

For all the harsh words
I hurled at you from
my own private pain
in order to also
make you ache.

Let compassion
enfold every cell
in my body
and seep into the deepest parts
of my soul.
Let it float down
gently like snowflakes
to settle on
every raw and exposed surface.

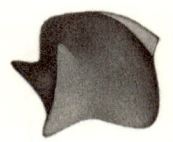

Retraining My Brain

So, I am retraining my brain.
Retraining my brain!
Scientists tell us
the brain can change,
new pathways are possible,
neurons that fire together,
wire together.

Teasing apart past associations
is hard work.
Each thought, every feeling
attached to something else,
heading down pathways
it's best not to go.
Ego rears its mangy head
and bellows loudly,
digging its claws in ever deeper,
not wanting to give up its hold.
It takes huge amounts of intention,
huge amounts of attention,
huge amounts of desire.

Retraining the brain entails setting up
new links and patterns,
pathways of goodness and happiness and calm,
seeing glimpses of yourself
that have been hiding
for way too long.

It's very hard work,
but I am feeling
brief flashes of joy,
increasing periods of ease,
daily gratitude.

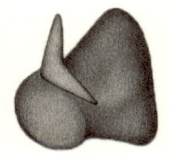

A Blank Page

Today is a blank page
calling out for clarity,
or insight or wisdom.
None of these today,
only thoughts swirling around each other,
feelings bubbling up from life's cauldron.

Our culture seems to have given up
seeking truth and valuing honesty,
relying on the loudest voice
or the biggest bully.
Meanwhile babies and children,
parents trying to give them a better life,
starve at our borders,
not allowed in, kept in cages.
And thousands sleep on our streets
while fat cats eat caviar and laugh
about their millions, their billions,
unable to stop grasping
at their angst-filled, unhappy lives.

Coronavirus rears its writhing head,
infiltrates another country,
and devours another life.
Fear swirls in its path as
citizens try to prepare
with masks and gloves
and sanitizers and plans,
unsure of what to do,
unsure of each other,
unsure of themselves.

Our planet mourns for itself
as we watch things begin to implode,
too little too late.
A grave mistake
thinking we are masters over all,
we watch as epic storms
and massive wildfires
show us who really knows.

These things are large,
beyond us we think.
We despair.
But we can impact this world
with our thoughts,
our words,
our actions.
All it takes is
seeing things as they are,
speaking the truth, and
moving through the world
with respect and appreciation.

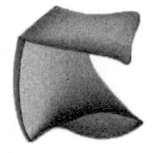

Free Stuff

What an easy way
to get rid of the stuff
I no longer want.
Just put it out at the curb.

The white-hot words
I said in anger,
the shroud of shame I've carried
over the years,
the ache of longing for things
to be different,
the ever-present push to be better,
the not holding
of this life, this day, this hour
as precious and fleeting.

With spaciousness and light
I see the free stuff in my life
    the rumble of thunder and
        flash of lightning,
    a huge golden moon just above the horizon
        floating in the dark, night sky,
    the cottonwoods swaying
        and rustling in the breeze,
    a goldfinch splashing
        in the birdbath,
    purple lupine blooming in the spring.

Blue Sky

I am the blue sky,
deep
wide open
steady
infinite.

Clouds form,
threaten
and then shift.
I am the container,
not the clouds.

I look up
and take a deep breath,
expand
beyond thoughts
of needing this or
pushing away that.
I merge with the sky
and float.

From above I see that
things are exquisite,
in need of care
and compassion,
so much beauty,
so much suffering.

And here I am,
here with myself.
What better thing
than to be
exactly who I am?

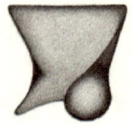

Landing Here

How did I land here
with this gentle, kind husband
authentic, unique children
a loyal family
and interesting friends
a healthy body and a curious mind
a safe, warm home
space to walk and wonder and breathe?

How was it that I landed
in my family of origin,
full of joy and light and love,
mischievous eyes and smiling mouth,
with a mother who wasn't ready,
a father who didn't see,
and older siblings who survived
as they needed to,
found their shaky paths,
as I hid and watched and was lost?

I could've landed
in any number of places
but I landed here.
Never hungry,
never physically unsafe,
never without everything I could need,
never completely alone.

Yet there has been
primal fear,
aching loneliness,
deep sadness and grief.

Why did I land here
in this life
at this time?

Indigenous People's Day

Today is Indigenous People's Day,
formerly known as Columbus Day.
I've done some reading, watched some movies,
and am beginning to understand
how important it is to get it right,
how those who write the history books
are the ones with power,
those who have a stake in
maintaining the view of the world they dominate,
hiding behind heroic words,
words that suppress what actually took place.

People that were living off the land
were in the way,
were convinced they needed contracts to
remain on the land
they'd honored for generations.
Colonizers came in with guns blazing,
bodies infected and
other strategies for destroying
those who were here.
They knew best.

And now it continues.
Where is the foundation of truth?
Choose whatever story you want,
whatever will promote your position,
tear down someone else's.
It's tribe against tribe,
winner takes all.

History is supposed to be a teacher.
Some days I can't see we've made much progress.

Breathe In

Breathe in.
Breathe out.

Breathe in, deeply and slowly.
Breathe out, all of the air.

Breathe in spaciousness.
Breathe out everything you don't need.

Breathe in love.
Breathe out fear, all of your fear.

Breathe in calm and peace.
Breathe out needing to know answers.

Breathe in courage.
Breathe out settling and complacency.

Breathe in forgiveness.
Breathe out judgment of yourself, of others.

Breathe in gratitude.
Breathe out wanting and whining.

Breathe in truth.
Breathe out easy answers and not thinking for yourself.

Breathe in patience.
Breathe out the need for control.

Breathe in strength.
Breathe out giving in and giving up.

Breathe in hope.
Breathe out the pull toward listlessness and lack of agency.

Breathe in what is here right now.
Breathe out everything else.

Breathe in love.
Breathe out love.

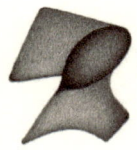

My Sister's Meditation

It was a course.
We were learning
our connection to nature,
that nature is kind,
how nature can heal.
Flowers with their ephemeral beauty,
trees and the memories they hold.

My meditation was for her,
and hers for me,
two sisters
enlisting the power of nature
for good.

There were hummingbirds
everywhere, she said,
sucking out the leukemia
cells whose development had been arrested
by the medications in my trial.
They were everywhere
sipping with their tiny tongues,
up to thirteen times a minute,
digesting all those cells and parts of cells
no longer needed, getting in the way.
A labor of love.

And when the hummingbirds
had finished their work,
a vast flock of butterflies
arose from my chest
and took flight,
wings of soft turquoise,
the orange of the sunset, and
the deep blue of the sky.
It was as if I too had been released
from worn out stories
and old identities,
illusions of limitation.
I soared free,
light as a butterfly's wing.

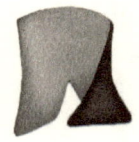

What I Do Know

That there is a certain point as the sun is setting when
the tops of the trees
or the snow on mountaintops
glow with dazzling pink.

That there is music that makes
tears well up and overflow,
with both a reaching out and
a turning in.

That the fragrance of freshly ground coffee
is heavenly as is
the first rich, hot sip every morning.

That dark chocolate with a bit of sea salt
is exquisite,
sweet balanced by a bit of tanginess.

That on certain days, at certain moments,
your face looks soft,
so soft and open
that looking into your eyes
I feel I can glimpse your soul.

That when I hold hands with you,
I feel like I'm home.

That when we dance,
and I am taken in your arms
and float across the floor,
swinging and whirling
through a familiar song,
it feels glamorous, intimate and right.

That a long, tight hug melts everything
that has happened,
or might have happened,
during that day.

That our three children
are people I respect
and admire,
love deeply,
that it was such great fortune that
these three were the ones who arrived!

That open-ended exchanges
about what I feel
and ponder
and long for, and
what things are on your mind,
what touches your heart,
what you yearn for,
bring me alive.

That reading a well-written book
with characters of depth and
a plot that urges me on,
or a book that teaches me
about people, or the world, or anything,
is a suspension of time and
a place of reverence.

That ferreting out weeds in the garden
makes me feel like it's easier to breathe.

That laughing hard,
tears-rolling-down-my-cheeks hard,
is the best.

That traveling to another country,
experiencing another culture,
gives me a sense of our differences
and how we are the same,
that space and time are illusion.
Interconnectedness
settles in my bones.

That I'm much less likely to look back with regrets
than to see that all that went before
as leading up to the bounty of the present.

That people are fascinating and generous
and frustrating and silly
and judgmental and insightful
and entertaining and compassionate,
just like me.

That my body is a challenge and a teacher.
Childbirth, broken bones,
surgeries, pain,
swimming and biking and hiking,
creating, holding and loving.
It is a constant companion,
a gift of presence.

That the truth is the truth.
There is no fabricating or stretching
or minimizing or denying.
The truth is the truth.

Much to Celebrate

Twentieth Anniversary

Vibrant blue eyes
clear and alive,
soft, full lips
to touch or kiss,
strong features
softened by time and experience and love.

Earthy chicken curry or
spicy chile rellenos
sturdy partitioned shelves
accompanist par excellence
master gardener
patient father
devoted husband
ever open to new ideas
and pursuits
alive in his life.

A body that envelops me
in comfort and warmth
scents of fresh air and work and passion
hands and arms that hold me gently
or explore with urgent need
caressing and discovering
each new texture
every contour and shape
an adventure of the senses
that leads us back to each other
submerged in this moment,
giver and receiver of this gift.

A relationship's journey of
ebbs and flows
highs and lows
riding the currents
with commitment and hope,
a delicate dance of discovery
an expedition into the unknown
and patience that allows
the rhythms to develop
and beauty to emerge.

Love is not a statement.
Love is a flow,
a river finding new shores
pushing the boundaries,
evolving with quiet strength.

Hold my hand as we walk
through this life
facing its challenges,
dancing to the moon,
and resting in each other's arms,
for you are my gift.

Fiftieth Birthday

50 years,
    600 months,
        18,250 days,
            438,000 hours,
                and 26,280,000 minutes
                    have now passed in my life on
                        this earth.

I still have the times
    we laughed until tears streamed down our cheeks,

and the times I picked up the phone and it was you
    when you didn't even know how much I needed you
    to call
    (or did you?)

and the times you thought of something I said or did
    and told me that you remembered it.

I've kept the times
    I came to your door
    and you welcomed me in,

the times I embraced so much of your pain
    that my stomach hurt and my chest grew tight,

and the times we explored what we believe
    or what we don't believe.

I've kept the times you cheerily told me the same thing
    2 or 3 or 4 times because I didn't remember
    that I'd already asked you the same thing,

and the times you sat with me in my pain and fear
    that was so large and clammy that
    it surrounded us with its darkness.
    But you stayed.

I still have the times I've read something to you
    that I wrote
    and you took it seriously and cried or smiled
    because I was able to tell you just how it was,

and the times you've told me what matters most to you,
    what makes you giddy or fiercely angry,
    what makes you sing,
    what you long for that you may never have.

I've kept the times you've remembered what I love,
    and the times we've not spoken a word
    but communicated far better with our eyes.

I know you think you are here to celebrate a milestone in my life,
    but really you are here because
    you are each part of who I am today.

A Toast to Dorothea

Here's to you, Auntie D,
to you
    standing youthful,
              exposed
  breasts
in front of a succession of
              open
                  doors,
furry, winged, wide-eyed
companion at your feet.
It must be your Birthday!
A toast to you,
to walking through
those doors
to what lay beyond.

Here's to Galesburg, Auntie D,
she couldn't contain you!
To New York and designs for Macy's swimsuits,
to Sedona's red rock splendor,
to Huismes and her fertile gardens,
and Seillans with the key-hole pool,
to Paris and Rue de Lille.
Here's to New York,
     a home to the last.

Here's to you, Auntie D,
to passion
        and Max!
To chess and work and play.
to all of it for
             one
                    hundred
                            one
                                  years.
To it all!

Here's to you, Auntie D,
and your wild,
            not-to-be-contained
     spirit.

To primitive thoughts seeping
    from ancient African masks,
to whimsical insects
    invited in to dine,
to chairs with soft tails,
to seeing an image of oneself
    through leafy vines on your bathroom mirror.

Here's to you, Auntie D,
to your mind (oh, that mind!)
to the fertile images
and playful figures engaged
    in various private acts,
to the ripe fruit of your poetry,
      bracing,
           intoxicating,
                true,
bubbling to the surface,
breathing life
        onto paper.

Here's to cookie time, Auntie D,
to Veuve Cliquot (nothing less!),
Goldfish and pistachios,
to holding court in pigtails
    tied with red yarn,
to tales of former lives
       of family, of friends, of travel
remembered in detail,
          more alive in the telling.
We listened
        and drank
you in.

Here's to you, Auntie D,
to a glimpse of the world
      through eyes never too old
to see clearly,
to hearing the rich music
         of your art,
to touching hidden places
         in our souls,
to being
    more
       than we ever were before
we knew you.

---

*Dorothea Tanning, 1910–2012. Painter, sculptor, poet, novelist, aunt.

The Gift of Ginny

I woke to your text
from just after midnight.
"Signed on to hospice
I have no strength at all
pain
used up all my meds."

I knew this day would come,
but so soon?
There are still stories to tell,
teachers' wisdom to contemplate,
issues to grow through,
laughter to share,
hugs to cherish.

Yet I wish you
peace
as you give in
to knowing
there is nothing else to try,
no special cocktails
to endure,
no diet schemes
to keep you well,
no struggle left to make.

I wish you
understanding
and acceptance
that all was tried,
that your heart
knows what is best,
that all will be well.

I wish you
ease
as your soul guides you
down this part of your path,
and deep rest
for your body, mind, and spirit,
the sure knowledge
that you are forever
held close.

You have given me
your complete acceptance,
your focus and attention,
your openness and trust,
your willingness to explore
all the unturned stones
in each of us,
your companionship
on this journey,
your love.

I have been touched
so deeply
that joy comes in,
gratitude is the container
for my grief,
and love is everywhere.

Threshold/Thirtieth Birthday

The next minute,
hour, day, year
await.

Overflow
with trilling birdsong,
the serenity of sunset,
and expectation of dawn,
the exquisite pain of longing,
the grieving for what will be lost,
the satisfaction of work well done,
the joy of deep connection,
the surprise
of the very smallest thing.

Events arrive,
welcome
or not,
and forge the alchemy
of stronger bones,
a more generous heart,
a more open mind.

This step
into the unknown,
mysterious and thrilling,
uneasy and awake,
awaits.

But you are ready
to meet all that comes,
you have yourself.

Unsuspecting, Unprepared

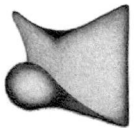

Gotta Get This Down

We heard about trouble in Wuhan, China:
people becoming sick,
being quarantined,
dying.
But that was so far away.

Then we watched it spread,
this coronavirus,
also known as COVID-19,
or SARS-CoV-2
from China to South Korea to Iran
on to Europe.

First cases in Seattle,
travelers in contact with each other,
quarantines for fourteen days,
careful tracing of social contacts.
More cases in other states,
new epicenter New York,
our global heart,
relentlessly spreading.
Cruise ships anchored offshore for fourteen days.

Fever, dry cough, fatigue.
Shortness of breath, inability to arouse,
chest pain, bluish lips or face, confusion.
We secretly check ourselves daily.
Safe, so far.

March 11 World Health Organization
declared COVID-19 a pandemic.
March 13 gatherings of 250 or more
strongly discouraged in MN,
fourteen total cases here.
March 16 restaurants, bars, museums closed,
now 54 cases, three via community transmission.
March 17 K-12 schools closed,
parents scramble to provide care.
March 23 no elective surgeries
allowed in our state.

Price gouging punishable by law,
protections discussed
for those who can't work at home or
are out of work.
Evictions not allowed,
support for small businesses
that had to close down.
Nothing untouched.

Gatherings of ten or fewer discouraged.
So hard to move away,
to create distance,
when what we want is to connect.

We have been home, only home
since March 13.
Streets are quieter,
parking lots empty.
People frantic to buy groceries
sign up for pick up or delivery.
No contact with friends,
concerts, plays, get-togethers canceled.
Social distancing,
no closer than six feet.
Wash your hands for twenty seconds minimum,
the length of "Happy Birthday."
Hand sanitizer home recipe thirty percent aloe vera,
    seventy percent alcohol.
Wipe all surfaces, wipe handles, wipe switches,
wipe grocery packaging, let mail or paper sit for hours.

We go out only to exercise,
to get fresh air and see the world.
But now in Italy,
poor sad Italy,
it's recommended that people not go out
even to exercise.
We are using the time
to clean,
to make photo books,
to read,
to do projects.
It's been less than two weeks.
We talk to our kids daily,
schedule video chats,
email.

The world has been swept by COVID-19,
experts have known this would occur
at some point, with some virus.
Not enough tests
so no real sense of numbers.
Shortages of personal protective equipment,
masks, gowns, gloves,
shortage of ventilators
for those who get very sick.
Decisions will have to be made.
Fifty percent of those on ventilators will live,
or die.

People are out of work,
voices of children
are heard during the day.
Stock markets plummet
and correct,
fears of recession.

A whole new language has arisen
COVID-19
self-quarantine
flatten the curve
PPE
social isolation
coronavirus
slip stream
shelter in place
virtual happy hours.

No end in sight,
we haven't peaked.
It's a bizarre horror film
that we are living.

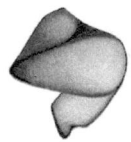

What Will Come of This Pandemic?

What will we learn
as we shelter inside,
our cars parked and
our credit cards in our wallets?
The skies are now clearer across the planet,
we may be learning what we can do without.

There is a quiet
from less traffic and bustle,
from taking the time
to make wise decisions
about our days.
Despite less
face-to-face interaction,
we may be more connected
with ourselves,
with each other,
with the planet.

Will we learn that systemic problems
only get worse in a crisis,
that the hungry just get hungrier,
the poor need even more,
the homeless still have nowhere to settle,
that all of them are prime targets for disease?
Will we learn to help them get what they need?

Will we come to value strong leadership
and sound science,
organization and well-thought-out plans?
Will we learn to plan ahead?

Will there be an understanding
that we need to work together,
that this threat touches us all
in the same ways,
that we are much stronger and resourceful
when we're united
than when we're divided?

Will we learn
to learn
from our experience,
rethink our relationship to the planet,
and how we use our resources,
how we take care of the less fortunate,
how we move through our days?

The Beforetime

Not so long ago
we greeted each other with hugs
or laid a gentle hand
on a friend's arm,
we sat closer than six feet
out of fondness and warmth,
companionship,
intimacy.

Not so long ago
we spoke words
with a different kind of worry
for how far their impact might spread,
rather than how they might
contaminate another's air.

And not so long ago
we didn't have to
worry about wearing masks,
and who was unwilling
and why,
what that meant
about our people
and who we are.

Not so long ago
people got dressed
to go out,
they headed to work,
and brought home paychecks
that covered what they needed
food, health care,
a roof over their heads,
the opportunity
to improve their chances.

Not so long ago
we visited
our friends and family,
and those who are lonely,
we spent time
in their physical presence
and comforted them
with our touch.

And not so long ago
we were completely free
to celebrate and honor
life's passages
in person,
graduations, weddings,
births and funerals,
holidays and birthdays.

Not long ago
we could dream
of travel
to visit family
or explore foreign lands.
Now we are most happy
to have a safe, warm
comfortable home.

We could take our time
at the grocery store,
or in line at the bank,
linger over dinner
shared with family or friends,
places of worship
and exercise centers
were not cause for concern.

Not so long ago
we didn't read
daily statistics
on how many
now have the virus,
we didn't have plans
for where we would quarantine
or how
if it came to our house,
we didn't know anyone
who had become ill
or died of this.

But not long ago
we did not know
to feel this grateful
for loved ones and their health,
for all the ways we can connect,
for simple pleasures
readily available in our homes,
and authors who write good books,
for a night's restful sleep,
for each day's dawning.

Lost and Found

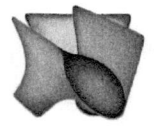

Child's Face

Transparent innocence,
expressions sweet and honest,
a face that perfectly manifests
who she is at this moment.

Skin so soft and smooth
that I long to brush against it.
Perfect curve of nose into cheek
and eye into nose,
impossible for my eyes
to trace those lines
often enough.

She glows from within,
such possibilities
of a life just on its way.
A wisp of hair dances
down one side of her face,
and I can barely contain
this surge of love and longing.

Butterfly in Chains

Aware
that it couldn't fly
where it desired to go
the butterfly tugged at its chains,
unconscious
of its bondage
until it spread its wings
to float up on the breeze.

Heavy shackles held
such a beautiful, delicate thing,
chained
for some unknown reason
to some unwanted past.
The butterfly accepted its burden,
embraced each day
as it was.

Now and then the butterfly
spread its wings
to ascend
where it was meant to go,
each attempt to soar
met by the unyielding chain.

In time
the butterfly realized
it could leave.
Spreading its wings,
and with great effort,
the butterfly loosed itself
from its chains
and floated up
with joy.

The butterfly had left part of itself
attached to the chain,
this fragment
no longer needed
in order to live.

Mindful or Mindless

Where was I today
>   while the world was waking to a new day
>   and the grass stretched toward the sun?

What did I see
>   while the blue of the sky grew ever more vivid
>   and the hibiscus unfurled its elegant petals?

What did I hear
>   as a child giggled uncontrollably
>   and the wren trilled its mating song?

What did I smell
>   while the fragrance of a single rose drew bees
>   from far and wide
>   and butter sizzled on freshly popped corn?

What did I taste
>   when a peach offered its sweet juice
>   or chocolate melted slowly on my tongue?

What did I feel
>   when you softly folded me in your strong arms
>   or when my feet were planted firmly on the
>   ground?

Where was I
>   while I thought I was living,
>   and got caught once again
>   filling up my days?

Where was I
while the present
marched into the future
and became the past,
forever lost?

Where am I now?

Reach Out

Reach out
to those you can't see, or hear, or touch,
reach out because you can feel
they are there.

Reach out to another
to see them
from where they stand,
knowing your perspective
is just the one you choose
to live in.

Reach out to another
to hear them laugh,
the universal language of joy and playfulness,
and reach out to hear them cry
because your soul has also known
sorrow and fear and pain.

Reach out in gratitude
that we stand firmly on the same ground,
that the air that caresses and sustains me
is the same air you breathe,
that the sky that inspires our dreams
holds us all,
that we are here at this important time together.

Reach out in love
because our differences are only there
when we believe they are,
because the energy of love connects us
across time and distance,
because love is the only way.

If I Should Die

If I should die,
    think of the exhilarating winds of January,
    their flush on my cheeks and
    strength at my back,

think of the moon in
    its pregnant golden
    fullness one night,
    its silvery whisper another,

think of an infant's face
    sweet and new,
    look into its eyes,
    its knowing eyes.

When I die,
    look for the lilies-of-the-valley
    pushing up
    through the soil, reaching
    toward the warm, spring sun,

and the faint pink
    of early dawn,
    dark trees silhouetted
    at the edge of the sky.

There I will be.

The Grace of Writing, a Sestina Practice

She was brought to the pen by a need
to put her pain, her life in words,
black pen on white paper recreating times
that begged for attention and light.
Hurt and pain transformed, became inspiration
and she finally saw it all as grace.

The physical act of writing is a graceful
process, words tumbling out of need
or flowing when one is inspired.
Thoughts, emotions become words
chosen to coax things from the dark and into the light.
For that soul it is time!

If the focus is our busy lives, our limited time,
questions arise, pulling us away from the grace
of difficulties understood, where dark turns to light
and we often write from a need
to fix our troubled views in words,
the process then less inspired.

Where do you search for inspiration?
Are you able to find enough time
so that your compositions aren't just words
and you somehow touch that sweet grace
where you might write from a place of need
but your soul creates pure light?

On occasion I've felt myself lighter
after penning a poem, somehow inspired
by experience, by sadness, joy or need.
I become unaware of time,
the act of writing filled with the grace
of sharing myself through words.

It's a funny thing about which words
we choose, exposing dark secrets or humor and light,
I stretch and reach for grace
but have found one can't demand inspiration,
it will arrive softly when I allow myself time
and marry easy flow to tortured need.

Writing, then, is the grace of the word
where one's pain, joy, or needs are prodded or eased
into the light,
and we become inspired, time after time.

*A sestina is a form originating in France consisting of six, 6-line, usually unrhymed stanzas in which the end words of the first stanza recur as the end words of the following five stanzas in a successively rotating order and as the middle and end words of the three verses of the concluding tercet.

Dad and Uncle Bill

In the middle of winter
on a crackling cold eve
two brothers were cruisin'
in their parents' old Chev.

There's nothin' like driving
and checking out the sights,
hometown boys in high school
on a still winter night.

Comin' back from the ice rink
and headed toward home
the car made up its mind,
it just wouldn't go.

So now they were stranded
right over the tracks
train whistle in the distance
approachin' real fast.

They ground on the starter
and pushed on the pedal
but nothing would happen,
they were stuck on the metal.

Some men came along
who noticed their plight
and they heaved and they pushed
with all of their might.

The train bore down on them
its whistle screamed a warning
the boys grew more frantic,
nothing was working.

The older of the brothers
came totally undone
while the others pushed and shouted,
he jumped up and down.

And just as it seemed
they'd next hear a crash
adrenaline and muscles
got the car off the tracks.

The impact on the elder
meant a week of mother's care.
As he lay home in bed,
she knew nothing of their scare.

When until a few days later
headlines hot off the press:
"Local Boys Have Narrow Escape!"
explained their frightful stress.

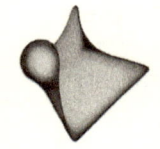

This Sadness

What is this sadness
that takes up residence
before I wake every morning,
weighing on my chest
as I come to the surface,
a shadowy presence
I can almost glimpse
at the periphery of my vision?

This sadness feels old,
stretching back
to the edges of memory,
part of my DNA.
Perhaps this is how I am made,
to start first from
heartbreak,
and injustice,
and loneliness in this world.

Is it all of the losses,
yours and mine,
the little disappointments,
or those so huge
they crack you open,
or those yet to come?

Is it scattered traces
of yesterday's news,
images of those desperate
to return to their homelands,
families with nowhere to stay,
without enough to eat?
Is it the guns everywhere?

I fill my lungs,
breathe deep this new day
and the sadness floats away
as if on the wings of a robin
returned to greet spring.

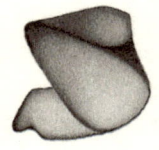

Graceport Walk

Back warmed by September's sun,
face touched softly by lake's playful breeze,
I walked the shore, and
felt pulled
        to look up and out, way out
        where thoughts lost
            their grip and
            sights became feelings.

Little Oak

The scraggly tree stands
small and gnarly
    bark sturdy against deep January's bite
        and late July's parching glare.

It stands alone, exposed
    no leaves.

Springtime's shy growth gives
    way to early summer's lush exuberance,
dogs race free
birds warble conversations
    about breakfasts of bright-colored berries.

And this tree waits.

When all around has stopped noticing,
    perhaps lost hope,
there is new growth
    healthy and green!

The little tree wasn't waiting;
    it had everything it needed
    and emerged in its own time.

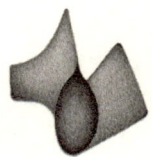

The Venus of Willendorf

Emerging out of stone
you've watched with us for millennia,
witness to our weary wayward world.

Thirty-thousand years of
                    memory
                            laughter,
                                    pain,
                                        hope,
                                            tears.

    Remind us
        that stone can be transformed
           into the softest of curves,
        that what has been lost
           can be found,
        that we must be ever ready
           to birth something new,
        that your most powerful alchemical gifts
           are patience and love.

*Found in 1908 in Willendorf, Austria, the Venus of Willendorf statue is 25,000 to 30,000 years old.

Snowfall

Snow floats down
as the earth waits,
each flake exquisite
soft
calm
silent,
muffling the sounds of a busy world.

Tree branches laden with fluff,
crab apples dangling since fall
wear little caps of white.
Houses clean and solid,
watch and wait.

We are safe and warm inside
where windows act as invitations
to the mystery of this pure white,
blanketing the earth
one flake at a time.

Brain's First Minute

Awake. Is this the day I give myself a break from those morning stretching exercises? The play last night, loved it. Do the actors have a hard time getting themselves up for every performance, day after day? Is it their belief in the message that makes their performances so authentic? Why did I say that to her in that tone of voice? Why did I say that at all? What will I make for dinner? Have to take the meat out of the freezer. Oh god, I remember driving by those vast feed lots in New Mexico, body wedged up against body, no space to stretch, no place to move. Not unlike how young black men are treated in this country, incarcerated to control, to get them off the streets. No freedom to move, no safe place to be. And the thousands of refugees, what choices do they have on this day? No space to move, no place to be themselves. The planet is confused, shattered. And here I lie in the safest place in the world. Time to get up.

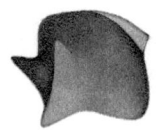

Morning Walk

The sun was just beginning
to rise above the trees,
my shadow was long
relaxed
its edges soft.
I followed where she led.

The birds a choir
singing
their tiny hearts out,
a glorious symphony of
gratitude, energy, joy.

The grasses were tall,
many up to my shoulders,
having started from nothing
this spring
pushing up
through fertile ground
just weeks ago.

And the trees,
Oh! The trees
grounded and majestic,
waxy leaves emerging
as the sun warmed their sap
and coaxed them to grow.

Wildflowers blanketed the fields
that ran along the path,
wild iris's deep purple,
hot pink of wild rose,
little white darlings,
yellow, shining stars,
bright orange clusters,
sweet pink clover.

After some time
I turned back,
sated with these gifts.
My shadow
followed me
and the choices
I will make for today.

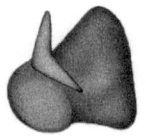

Meditation

This morning I lay on my cushioned exercise pad
in the pre-dawn shadows,
head on a flowered pillow,
body covered with a soft down puff,
and played a gorgeous CD.

Rich notes instantly
permeated my body
and infused my cells,
vibrated in sweet response
to landscapes of expansive power and beauty,
melodies of exquisite heartache,
chords of quiet peace.

Every cell craved this communion,
became the music.
Blessed gift.
Reconnected, realigned.

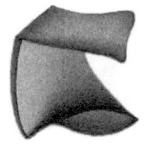

Mid-October Day

As I sit and gaze out my window
the orange leaves on our Korean Sun Pear
are on fire,
the purple mum is completely full of itself,
and the cottonwoods are fluttering in the wind.
The grass is emerald green after last night's rain
and the spike in the middle of a summer planter
still stands tall.
The Norway pines wave their droopy arms
and frisky red ground squirrels
scamper across the fence top
filling their coffers with red Haralson apples
dropped from our tree.
The sky is blue and wide open,
the air fresh and clean.

What more do I need?

Beauty

Reflects
wonder,
innocence,
gratitude,
elegance,
mystery,
awe,
purity,
the beholder.

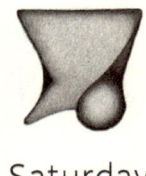

Saturday

The washing machine
made a loud, clunking noise,
and when I opened the door
clouds of white smoke billowed out.

I considered
how things change
one minute
to the next,
how change
is part of daily life
catching us a bit off guard
or shifting the whole
trajectory of our lives.

I understand
these little shifts,
events,
cataclysms
can't be helped
predicted
controlled.
What remains a challenge
is knowing
I have power,
the power to choose
how I will respond.

The washing machine's implosion
was a minor annoyance.
Who knows what tomorrow will bring?

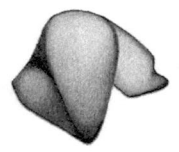

Home

Just yesterday
I was baking,
baking Christmas cookies
to deliver or send.

Beautiful music
from the stereo,
body swaying,
hands shaping.

At one moment
I was overcome,
eyes filled.
Such joy.
Knowing and peace
and joy.

It was about coming home.
It was about love.

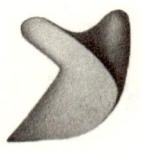

Black Cotton Dress

It was the first time
I went out
a month after
giving birth
to you.
Wedding of a colleague,
I wore a black cotton dress
trimmed with borders of
gray-blue and burgundy.

My mind touched lightly on
your sweet, chubby body
alert dark eyes
the little snuffling sounds
you would make
as you tried to locate
my nipple.
As I listened and watched
the joining of two,
I thought about you,
felt that stirring warmth
and soaked the front
of my black cotton dress.

I ache for those quiet nights
when I lifted you up
and held you close,
no space between
our bodies,
the house settled and still
your little body
relaxed and sleepy,
back when I was able
to give you everything
you needed.

www.ingramcontent.com/pod-product-compliance
Lightning Source LLC
Chambersburg PA
CBHW020534080526
44583CB00013B/858